THE ISLAMIC FAITH

ABDULAZIZ AL-TARIFI

فصول في العقيدة

(الرسالة الشامية)

المؤلف
عبد العزيز بن مرزوق الطريفي

ترجمة وتحرير
عادل صلاحي

ENGLISH
إنجليزي

Osoul Center

This book has been conceived, prepared and designed by the Osoul Centre. All photos used in the book belong to the Osoul Centre. The Centre hereby permits all Sunni Muslims to reprint and publish the book in any method and format on condition that 1) acknowledgement of the Osoul Centre is clearly stated on all editions; and 2) no alteration or amendment of the text is introduced without reference to the Osoul Centre. In the case of reprinting this book, the Centre strongly recommends maintaining high quality.

  +966 11 445 4900

  +966 11 497 0126

  P.O.Box 29465, Riyadh 11457

  osoul@rabwah.sa

  www.osoulcenter.com

In the Name of God,
the Lord of Grace, the
Ever Merciful

Table of Contents

Introduction		7
Chapter 1	Islam is the religion of all prophets and the true and everlasting religion.	11
Chapter 2	Interpretation of Islam: What is in God's book may be interpreted only through the Sunnah, the understanding of the Prophet's companions and analogy with these.	13
Chapter 3	The right owed to God by His servants: Unbelievers incur punishment in hell but this does not negate granting them benefits in this life.	15
Chapter 4	Faith, disbelief and hypocrisy: Which property enjoys sanctity? – Who is considered unbeliever? – The status of ignorant people whether deliberately or by inability.	14
Chapter 5	The nature of faith: What is faith? – Faith may increase or decrease. – What proves it and who has excuses.	21
Chapter 6	God's names and attributes: Their confirmation or negation. – God's will. – Are His attributes comparable with those of others?	25
Chapter 7	God's words and the Qur'an: The Qur'an is His word, whether spoken or written. – The ruling regarding anyone who claims that it is a creature.	27
Chapter 8	The nature of religious truth: The relation between religious text and reason.	
Chapter 9	God's legislation for religion and life: Both are the same. – God's law is suited for all generations. – Deduction of rulings is only in cases where no religious text applies.	29
Chapter 10	God's determination of destiny: His will and cause and effect.	31
Chapter 11	The inevitability of death: Resurrection, reckoning, reward and punishment, and other matters related to the life to come.	33 35
Chapter 12	The Muslim community: Its leader and the obedience due to him. – Conditions of his authority and the ruling regarding rebellion. – What is due to him from his people and the place of scholars.	37
Chapter 13	Jihad: Its types and conditions. – Intention and obedience of the leader of the Muslim community.	39
Chapter 14	The status of the Prophet's companions and their distinction: The best of them and the consequences of speaking ill of them. – How to regard their disagreements.	41
Chapter 15	Who may be ruled as unbeliever and on what basis: The claim that a particular person will be in heaven or hell.	43
Chapter 16	Servitude and the nature and extent of freedom.	45

PREFACE

All praise is due to God who has bestowed this book from on high on His servant, and has ensured that it remains free of distortion, unerringly straight, meant to warn people of a severe punishment from Himself, and to give the believers who do good works the happy news that they shall have a goodly reward which continues to be theirs forever. Furthermore, it warns those who assert, 'God has taken to Himself a son.' No knowledge whatever have they of Him, and neither had their forefathers. Dreadful indeed is this saying that issues from their mouths. Nothing but falsehood do they utter. (The Qur'an: 18: 1-5) Our Lord, bestow peace and blessings on Prophet Muhammad and his wives the Mothers of Believers, his offspring and members of his household as you had bestowed peace and blessings on Abraham and his household. You are indeed worthy of all praise, infinite in Your glory.

This book is a short outline of the Islamic faith as held by the Sunni Muslim community. The author dedicates this work to the people of Syria – may God put an end to their distress – and to Muslims in general. He gives this outline guided by the Qur'an and the Prophet's sunnah, as well as the faith expounded by the early Muslims, i.e. the Prophet's companions and the generation of *tabi'in* who succeeded them. As the author has an excellent command of Arabic, the book benefits by clarity of expression enabling the reader to easily comprehend the true Islamic faith.

The true faith is the foundation of good action that benefits the one who does it in this present life and in the life to come. It is also the starting point from which the world Muslim community may reclaim its leading position in the world which it deserves. It is only natural, therefore, that scholars should dedicate themselves to explaining and clarifying the true faith. In doing so, they also point out what is in conflict with it, or mars its beauty, of word and deed.

We pray to God to benefit our Muslim brethren by this book and to reward its author, translators, publishers and those who have helped to produce it. May they benefit by this reward when they meet their Lord on the Day of Judgement.

All praise is due to God, the Lord of all the worlds

Osoul Center

INTRODUCTION

*P*raise be to God who deserves all praise. Every good thing comes from Him and to Him all thanks are due. I bear witness that there is no deity other than Him: Nothing is equal or comparable to Him and He has no partners. I also bear witness that Muhammad is God's servant and messenger. Peace and God's blessings be upon him, members of his household and his companions.

This is a brief presentation of the Islamic faith. I would like to address in particular the people of Syria as they strive to regain their country and homeland after it has been colonised for nearly a century, first by Christians then by sects that adopt esoteric beliefs. As a result, deviation and alteration has occurred in many fundamental and secondary aspects of Islam.

A number of people from Syria and elsewhere have asked me to write for them the answers to the questions that everyone will be asked on the Day of Judgement in relation to what is due to God from His servants. This is the essence of what God commanded Noah and all of the prophets that succeeded him, and took its final form with the message of Islam delivered to the unlettered Prophet Muhammad (peace be upon him). 'In matters of faith, He has ordained for you the same as He had enjoined on Noah – that which We have revealed to you [Muhammad] – and as We enjoined on Abraham, Moses and Jesus: "Steadfastly uphold the faith and do not divide into factions"'. (42: 13)

With the increase of desires and gains to be coveted, leanings diverged and this led to a variety of views being put forward, which in turn led to the emergence of various groups and sects. In addition, knowledge of Arabic weakened among Arabs and other communities and it became easier to convince people of some outlandish interpretations and to raise doubts about certain beliefs. As a result it became easier to justify these beliefs on the basis of wrong interpretations of Qur'anic verses and statements by the Prophet. If this was easy to achieve by various groups in the first century of Islam and in subsequent centuries, it is all the easier for those who came later, provided that desire and doubt exist. In fact, a doubt begins as a desire leading to the expression of doubt before it becomes a trend to be followed. People then accept it blindly without knowing its origin. God says: 'Why is it that every time a messenger comes to you with a message that does not suit your fancies, you glory in your arrogance, charging some (messengers) with lying and slaying others?' (2: 87) He talks in the beginning of people's fancies, leading to an arrogance that later becomes disbelief and enmity. This is how deviant trends and ideas start in any community.

God revealed the truth and right guidance to His messenger, Muhammad (peace be upon him). Whoever wants guidance in its pure form must take it from its origins, without any addition of the ideas of people that may detract from this purity. Revelation may be likened to water and people's minds like containers. God sent down His revelation and put it in the Prophet's heart. The Prophet passed it on to his companions and they gave it to their successors, the *tabi*[*in*. But as revelation is passed from one stage to the next it becomes less pure. The best and purest containers were the first ones: the Prophet, then his companions. Muslim relates in his S*a*hih anthology of *hadiths*: 'Abu Musa reports that the Prophet said: "I am a safeguard for my companions: when I am gone, my companions will face what is in store for them. My companions are safeguards for my community: when they are gone, my community will face what is in store for it"'.

Faith may only be taken from God's revelations in His book, the Qur'an, and the Prophet's Sunnah: 'It is He who has sent to the unlettered people a messenger from among themselves to declare to them His revelations, to purify them and to instruct them in the Book and in wisdom'. (62: 2) Any religious knowledge that does not come from these two sources is ignorance.

The most accurate understanding of God's revelations is that of the Prophet's companions. We shall mention what His revelations impart and what was understood by the Prophet's companions and agreed by their generation, the best of all generations.

CHAPTER ONE

Islam[1] is the only divine faith. God does not accept anything else from any one of His servants, be they human or jinn. He says: 'He who seeks a religion other than self-surrender to God, it will not be accepted from him'. (3: 85) 'The only true faith acceptable to God is [man's] self-surrender to Him'. (3: 19)

Islam is the faith preached by all prophets. God says: 'Before your time We never sent a messenger without having revealed to him that there is no deity other than Me. Therefore, you shall worship Me alone'. (21: 25) 'We have sent revelations to you just as We sent revelations to Noah and the prophets after him; as We sent revelations to Abraham, Ishmael, Isaac, Jacob and their descendants, Jesus, Job, Jonah, Aaron and Solomon, and as We vouchsafed to David a Book of divine wisdom, and as [We inspired other] messengers whom We have mentioned to you previously, as well as other messengers whom We have not mentioned to you. And God has spoken His word directly to Moses. [These] were messengers sent to bring good news and to give warning, so that people may have no argument against God once these messengers [had come]. God is almighty, wise'. (4: 163–5) In another surah God mentions by name the following prophets: Noah, Abraham, Isaac, Jacob, David, Solomon, Job, Joseph, Moses, Aaron, Zachariah, John, Jesus, Elijah, Ishmael, Elisha, Jonah and Lot. He then says: 'Those are the ones whom God has guided. Follow, then, their guidance'. (6: 90)

The religions of all prophets are the same in their fundamental concepts and principles, but they vary in some details, but not all. So, details may be different but the fundamentals are the same. Both Moses and Jesus were sent with divine messages to the Children of Israel. As God gave the Gospel to Jesus as His message, He abrogated some of the rules that were in the Torah revealed to Moses. Defining his message, Jesus said to his people: 'And [I have come] to confirm that which has already been sent down of the Torah and to make lawful to you some of the things which were forbidden you. I have come to you with a sign from your Lord; so remain conscious of God and obey me'. (3: 50) Both prophets, Moses and Jesus, were sent to the same community yet some of the details of their messages differed. All the more reason that other messages may have differences in detail as well.

---

1 The linguistic meaning of Islam is 'self-surrender, submission, etc.'

Every divine law suffered distortion and alteration. God says: 'There are some among them who twist their tongues when quoting the Scriptures, so that you may think that [what they say] is from the Scriptures when it is not from the Scriptures. They say: "It is from God", when it is not from God. Thus, they deliberately say of God what they know to be a lie'. (3: 78) 'They take (revealed) words out of their context'. (4: 46)

Thus people could not know the truth as God revealed it. The proper way to correct the situation was to send a new prophet. Hence, God re-established His true faith with the prophethood of Muhammad (peace be upon him). This meant that there is no true self-surrender to God and no true faith except that of Prophet Muhammad: 'He who seeks a religion other than self-surrender to God, it will not be accepted from him, and in the life to come he will be among the lost'. (3: 85)

God gave His message to all communities: Arabs and non-Arabs; human and jinn: 'We have sent you to all mankind so that you bring them good news and give them warning'. (34: 28) In an authentic *hadith*, Abu Hurayrah reports that the Prophet said: 'By Him who holds Muhammad's soul in His hand, any human being, Jew or Christian, who hears of me but dies without believing in that with which I have been sent shall be among the people of the Fire'.[2] God has guaranteed to keep the Qur'an safe from distortion and alteration. He says: 'It is We Ourselves who have bestowed this reminder from on high, and it is We who shall preserve it intact'. (15: 9)

---

2   Related by Muslim, 153.

CHAPTER TWO

No one may interpret Islam and how God wants it to be except God Himself, in his book, the Qur'an, and in the Sunnah of the Prophet. No human being has a higher status than God's Prophet, yet he only delivers what God reveals to him. God says: 'Messenger, proclaim what has been revealed to you by your Lord'. (5: 67) As he delivers his message, the Prophet also has to explain it and make it clear, as God says: 'The Messenger is not bound to do more than clearly deliver his message'. (24: 54) The explanation and clarification also comes from God as He says in reference to the Qur'an: 'When We recite it, follow its recitation. Then it will be for Us to make its meaning clear'. (75: 18–19)

The Sunnah is revelation from God to His messenger: 'He does not speak out of his own fancy. That [which he delivers to you] is nothing less than a revelation sent down to him'. (53: 3–4) When a question was put to the Prophet he would respond if the answer had been revealed to him. Otherwise, he would wait for the answer in new revelation.

The people who were closest to understanding what the Prophet said were his companions and their understanding of the Qur'an is clear evidence. Other than God, whoever says that anyone has the authority to state what is permissible or forbidden in religion claims a partnership with God in His rulings. This is blatant disbelief in God and an act of associating partners with Him. There is no disagreement among scholars on this.

When God revealed His book, His words carry meanings that He wanted to convey. The meanings He intended are explained only by Him and whoever of His creation is permitted to do so. A scholar who studies the Qur'an may deduce its meanings, provided he observes two conditions:
1. He sticks to the Arabic language and its grammar.
2. He does not contradict a clear meaning that is already established in the Qur'an.

Not everything that is attributed to God actually comes from Him. Followers of earlier divine messages went astray when they made arbitrary deductions, twisting what is definitive in order to contradict what is equivocal. God says of them: 'There are some among them who twist their tongues when quoting the Scriptures, so that you may think that [what they say] is from the Scriptures, when it is not from the Scriptures. They say: "It is from God", when it is not from God. Thus, they deliberately say of God what they know to be a lie'. (3: 78) Thus, they twisted the words when quoting 'the Scriptures' and their aim was to make you 'think that [what they say] is from the Scriptures' because it is very close to it. They did this with a definite aim to lead people astray.

CHAPTER THREE

It is God's right to be the only one offered all types of worship. He says: 'Your God is the One God: there is no deity but He, the Lord of Grace, the Ever Merciful'. (2: 163) It is His right that no one else should be associated with Him in any act of worship, whether mental, verbal or physical. He says: 'Worship God alone and do not associate any partners with Him'. (4: 36)

Associating partners with God obliterates every good action a human being does. God says to the Prophet: 'It has been revealed to you, and to those before you, that if you ever associate partners with God all your works shall certainly come to nothing and you shall certainly be among the lost'. (39: 65) These are God's words to Prophet Muhammad (peace be upon him) and they certainly apply to everyone else.

God does not forgive the association of partners with Him unless one genuinely repents: 'For a certainty God does not forgive that partners are associated with Him. He forgives any lesser sin to whomever He wills'. (4: 48) 'Those who disbelieve and bar others from the path of God, and in the end die unbelievers, shall not be granted forgiveness by God'. (47: 34)

Whoever dies an unbeliever will be in the Fire. God says: 'Whoever of you renounces his faith and dies an unbeliever, his works shall come to nothing in this world and in the world to come. Such people are destined for hell, wherein they shall abide'. (2: 217) 'Those who reject the faith and die unbelievers shall incur the curse of God, the angels and all mankind'. (2: 161)

An unbeliever may bring benefit to people during his life, which is something God enables him to do as He brings about all types of benefit to His creation. He makes the sun, the moon, winds, clouds, etc. yield their benefit, which is greater, to mankind. To disbelieve is to reject God, not nature; and God's punishment of an unbeliever is for denying God His rights, not denying the rights of nature.

CHAPTER FOUR

Belief and disbelief are cases that are determined by God alone. No one may be called an unbeliever without clear evidence from God. In their life on earth people are divided into two categories: believers and unbelievers. God says: 'It is He who has created you, yet some of you are unbelievers and some do believe'. (64: 2) Rulings that apply to them are those which God has revealed in His book, the Qur'an, and in the Prophet's Sunnah.

A hypocrite is treated according to what he does and says in public, which means that he is treated like the rest of Muslims and what they do and say. Hypocrites are of two types:

1. Unbelievers who harbour disbelief but pretend to believe. Thus, a hypocrite may pretend to believe in God, His messenger and book while in reality he denies them all. This is the worst type of hypocrisy.
2. Muslims who pretend to obey God but secretly intend to disobey Him. An example is a person who pretends to be true to his pledges but secretly resolves to break them. He may pretend to speak the truth but entertains the opposite thoughts and opinions, which is the lesser type of hypocrisy.

The basic rule is that the life and property of a believer are protected and unlawful to anyone. With regard to an unbeliever, they have no such protection. However, this does not apply universally and to all. An unbeliever may have protection because of his pledges or his promise of security and loyalty. On the other hand, a believer may be killed for an offence he commits, such as murdering someone or adultery when he is married.

No one is to be considered an unbeliever except those whom God and His messenger pronounced as such. For example:
- A person who denies God or His messenger (peace be upon him).
- A person who ridicules either God or His messenger. God says: 'Should you question them, they will say: "We have only been indulging in idle talk and jesting." Say: "Was it, then, at God, His revelations and His Messenger that you have been mocking? Make no excuses. You have disbelieved after you have professed to be believers." Though We may pardon some of you, We shall punish others, on account of their being guilty'. (9: 65–6)
- A person who in all arrogance refuses to submit to God and His messenger.

- A person who denies a definitive Islamic ruling.
- One who invents a falsehood and attributes it to God. God says: 'It is only those who do not believe in God's revelations that invent falsehood. It is they indeed who are liars'. (16: 105) 'Who commits a greater injustice than one who invents lies against God or denies the truth when it reaches him? Is not hell the proper abode for the unbelievers?' (29: 68) As used in this verse, and similar ones, injustice is synonymous with disbelief.
- One who offers worship to anyone other than God. He says: 'He that invokes besides God any other deity – a deity for whose existence he has no evidence – shall be brought to account before his Lord. Most certainly, the unbelievers shall never be successful'. (23: 117) This is applicable whether his worship is completely addressed to any being other than God or he considers those to whom he addresses his worship intermediaries between him and God. God says: 'They worship side by side with God what can neither harm nor benefit them, and say: "These will intercede for us with God." Say: "Do you presume to inform God of something in the heavens or on earth that He does not know? Limitless is He in His glory and exalted above whatever they may associate with Him"'. (10: 18)
- One who ascribes to others than God what belongs to God alone, such as God's right to legislate and rule. Such a person may describe without authority things as permissible or forbidden. The issuance of legislation and giving rulings are called by God as acts of worship. God says: 'All judgement rests with God alone. He has ordained that you should worship none but Him'. (12: 40)
- One who claims that anyone other than God has knowledge of what belongs to *ghayb*, i.e. what lies beyond the reach of creatures' perception, such as those who practise magic or astrology. God says: 'None in the heavens or earth knows what is hidden except God'. (27: 65)
- One who claims that anyone other than God has the power to create or control the universe, or cause life or death. God says: 'Do they assign to God partners that have created the like of His creation, so that both creations appear to them to be similar? Say: "God is the Creator of all things. He is the One who has power over all things"'. (13: 16)
- The same applies to anyone who takes unbelievers as allies instead of believers, and addresses his love and support to them. God says: 'Whoever of you allies himself with them is indeed one of them'. (5: 51)

Whoever is able to know and understand Islam but chooses to disregard it and turn away from it is an unbeliever, even though he is really unaware of it. The fact is that his ignorance of Islam is easy for him to remove. Therefore, God says in description of unbelievers: 'But nay, most of them do not know the truth, and so they stubbornly turn away'. (21: 24) The verse clearly mentions that they are ignorant, even though by choice. He also says: 'Yet the unbelievers ignore the warnings they have been given'. (46: 3) If a person remains ignorant of the details of the truth because he turned away when it was presented, this cannot be an excuse. In fact it is the reason that most people go astray. They learn some of it then turn away, unwilling to learn its details.

Most unbelievers pay little heed to proofs that are in the universe around them and in religious sources. God says: 'Yet many are the signs in the heavens and the earth which they pass by, paying no heed to them'. (12: 105) 'Nay, We have given them all that brings them glory. Yet from this their glory they turn away'. (23: 71) Turning away from learning the whole when one knows a part does not remove people's rights in their dealings with one another. How can it remove God's rights?

If we do not contemplate God's signs when we see them we are bound to miss their purpose. The quicker we turn away the more we miss. Thus we do not benefit by them even though the proof they provide is clear and powerful, and observed every day: 'We have set up the sky as a well-secured canopy. Yet they stubbornly turn away from all its signs'. (21: 32)

When man thinks that his turning away from the details of the truth and putting them behind him exempts him from what they entail, he is grossly mistaken. Turning away from the truth is motivated either by arrogance or by one's preference for play and pleasure. Hence, when he faces catastrophes and his pleasure is lost, he may realise the truth and revert to it.

CHAPTER FIVE

Taken together, words, action and belief constitute faith. Maghrib prayer consists of three *rak[ahs* and if one is not included, the prayer is not Maghrib. By the same token if any of the three elements: words, action and belief is lacking, the condition is not called faith.

The truth of these three constituents; words, action and belief, which when one is missing faith is missing, is a unique aspect of the religion advocated by Prophet Muhammad (peace be upon him). What is meant by 'belief' is not merely to love what is good for all people and to be free of hatred. This is something that most people would prefer, even though they may not believe in the Creator. What is meant by 'belief' in this context is what the mind says and does. What the mind should say is that it believes there is no deity other than God and that Muhammad is God's messenger, and that what Prophet Muhammad told us from his Lord is the truth. The mind's action is the love of God, His messenger and Islam. It also includes loving what God and His messenger love and to be sincere in one's worship of God.

The 'words' constituent of faith is not limited to what is generally accepted as 'good words', such as telling the truth, speaking kindly to one's parents, greeting people, showing the way to anyone who is lost, etc. These are matters that everyone loves, including unbelievers who deny God's existence. What is meant by 'words' are those words that are special to Muhammad's message. The most important of these are the declaration of God's oneness and that Muhammad is His messenger, and glorification of God.

Nor is the 'action' constituent limited to general 'good actions', such as dutifulness to one's parents, removing harmful objects from people's way, feeding the poor and needy, supporting those suffering injustice, being hospitable to one's guests, and so on. Again, people love such actions regardless of whether they are believers or not. What is meant here is the sort of action that Prophet Muhammad (peace be upon him) particularly outlined, such as prayer, zakat, fasting, the pilgrimage, etc.

Good actions, that all divine messages and human nature have outlined, such as to love what is good for all people, speaking the truth, dutifulness to parents, feeding the poor, removing harmful objects from people's way, etc. increase faith when they are offered for God's sake. However, their absence does not negate faith in the same way as practising them does not mean that the person doing them is a believer. All they prove is that the one who does them enjoys an upright nature. The nature that God equipped people with remains the same, close to accepting the truth: 'Set your face steadily towards the true faith, turning away from all that is false, in accordance with the natural disposition which God has installed into man. Nothing can change God's creation'. (30: 30)

Faith may increase or decrease and may be removed altogether. It is increased by practising what the religion prescribes and recommends and it is decreased by committing sin. It is not removed except by disbelief and associating partners with God. He says: 'True believers are only those whose hearts are filled with awe whenever God is mentioned, and whose faith is strengthened whenever His revelations are recited to them'. (8: 2) 'The believers may grow yet more firm in their faith'. (74: 31) 'It is He who sent down tranquillity into the hearts of the believers, so that they may grow more firm in their faith'. (48: 4)

No one's belief is confirmed after one has been unbeliever except by:
- Belief, which combines the mind's word and acceptance of the divine message with the mind's action, which is to love God and His messenger and to love what God and His messenger love;
- Declaration by word of mouth; and
- Physical action.

Whoever mentally accepts the faith and is able to make the verbal declaration but does not do so is not a believer. Similarly, a person who mentally accepts the faith and utters the verbal declaration and is able to do the actions that are peculiar to the Islamic faith but does not do them is also not a believer.

On the other hand, whoever wants to utter the declaration, or to do the action, but is unable to accomplish his purpose falls under what God says: 'God does not charge a soul with more than it can bear'. (2: 286) 'God does not burden anyone with more than He has given them'. (65: 7)

If a Muslim does something that annuls his faith, whether verbal, physical or mental, his faith is totally annulled. As we have said, words, action and belief together constitute faith and are compared to the three *rak[ahs* of Maghrib. If a worshipper does something that invalidates his prayer in one *rak[ah* the whole prayer is invalidated, even though he might have prayed the other *rak[ahs* well, without anything to invalidate them. This does not contradict what we have said that faith increases with offering more of what Islam requires and decreases with committing sinful actions, be they less or more serious. Likewise, the fact that all of a prayer is rendered invalid by doing one thing that is contrary to it does not contradict that it is greater and better when more of its good action is done, such as longer recitation of the Qur'an, stillness and glorification of God. It is a lesser prayer, but not invalid, if one does what is discouraged, such as looking to the sky during prayer or stretching one's arms on the floor when entering the prostration position, like dogs do. Nothing invalidates faith except what God has stated, in the same way that nothing invalidates prayer except what God has defined.

CHAPTER SIX

God has beautiful names and fine attributes. No one knows Him better than He knows Himself. Therefore, we deny what He has denied of Himself and confirm what He has confirmed in His book and His messenger's Sunnah. We say, in general, that every negative thing is inapplicable to Him and we confirm to Him in detail every attribute of perfection. We do not try to assign any form or likeness to Him and we do not compare Him to anyone or anything.

If anyone attributes to Him any negative thing in detail, we deny it in detail, just like He has denied that He ever had a wife or a son. He said: 'How can He have a child when He has never had a consort?' (6: 101) 'He begets none, nor is He begotten'. (112: 3) He also denied what the Jews said when they accused him of miserliness: 'The Jews say: "God's hand is shackled!" It is their own hands that are shackled. Rejected [by God] are they for what they say. Indeed, both His hands are outstretched. He bestows [His bounty] as He wills'. (5: 64)

We accept what is stated in God's revelations, such as God's names and attributes. We confirm the truth of these and understand some of their effects but do not go beyond that because nothing is comparable to God. He says of Himself: 'Nothing bears even the slightest comparability to Him. He alone hears all and sees all'. (42: 11)

In regard to His attributes, it is wrong to draw an analogy between God and anything whatsoever. Any analogy requires two parties: main and secondary. God is one without comparison, hence there is neither a secondary to draw close to Him nor a main to compete with Him. He is the One and only God, the Eternal, the Absolute. He begets none, nor is He begotten, and there is nothing that could be compared to Him.

The human mind is like a machine created by God: it compares what it hears to what it sees. It listens to what God tells us of Himself and because He is unseen the mind compares Him to the closest object it has seen. Every mind imagines His attributes according to what it has seen before and develops its understanding on this basis. However, God is without compare in all minds, therefore we must not negate any of His names or attributes because of any bad comparison people might have expressed. This is a case of negating the comparison by negating the attribute or His name. If we do so we commit the error of negating an invalid comparison and denying a true statement. What we should negate is the bad meaning that people might have expressed while confirming what God has stated of His names and attributes, without adding anything. God says: 'He knows all that lies open before them and all that is hidden from them, whereas they cannot have thorough knowledge of Him'. (20: 110) 'No power of vision can encompass Him, whereas He encompasses all vision; He is above all comprehension, yet is All-Aware'. (6: 103)

God is established on the Throne of His Almightiness in heaven. He says: 'He is the First and the Last, the Outer and the Inner. He has full knowledge of all things. It is He who created the heavens and the earth in six days and established Himself on the throne. He knows all that goes into the earth and all that comes out of it; all that descends from the skies and all that ascends to them. He is with you wherever you may be; and God sees all that you do'. (57: 3–4)

God thus confirms His establishment and His knowledge of all things. He tells us that He is always with His servants with His knowledge, hearing and sight. As He says: 'He is with you wherever you may be'. (57: 4) In the case of the believers, He is with them in all these respects as well as with His support and care. Just like He said to Moses and Aaron: 'Have no fear. I shall be with you. I hear all and see all'. (20: 46)

God's will is complete and embraces everything: whatever He wills is realized and whatever He does not will shall never take place. We confirm this as He has stated it without engaging in any further discussion. Unlike rationalists, who try to speak about impossibilities and combining what are mutually contradictory, etc. God says: 'He answered: "Thus it is. God does what He wills"'. (3: 40) 'But God does whatever He wills'. (2: 253) 'Lord of the Throne, the Glorious, He does whatever He wills'. (85: 15–16)

We confirm all His names and attributes that are stated in His revelation and stop at that. We also negate the negative qualities that reason indicates to be inapplicable to Him even though they are not stated, such as grief, weeping, hunger, etc.

CHAPTER SEVEN

The Qur'an is God's word: He truly said it in sounds, words and surahs. We do not say that 'it is mere meaning without utterance', but we say that God speaks whenever He wills: 'God has spoken His word directly to Moses'. (4: 164) 'When Moses came for Our appointment and his Lord spoke to him'. (7: 143) His word is what He says: 'God says the truth and He alone shows the right path'. (33: 4)

God's word is memorized in people's hearts: 'Nay, but this [Qur'an] consists of verses that are clear to the hearts of those gifted with real knowledge'. (29: 49) It is heard with people's ears: 'If any of the idolaters seeks asylum with you, grant him protection so that he may hear the word of God and then convey him to his place of safety'. (9: 6) The fact that it was God's messenger who delivered it to us does not alter the fact that it is God's own word.

It is written down as God says: 'By a scripture inscribed on unrolled parchment'. (52: 3) God has preserved it on a tablet He has kept: 'This is indeed a glorious Qur'an, inscribed on an imperishable tablet'. (85: 21–2) 'It originates in the source of revelation kept with Us; it is indeed sublime, full of wisdom'. (43: 4) The fact that it is written down does not alter the fact that it is God's word, since paper is created like ink is created. God says: 'Even if We had sent down to you a book written on paper and they had touched it with their own hands'. (6: 7) He thus makes the book and the paper two different things.

Confirming that the Qur'an is His own word, even though it is written with created pens and created ink, He says: 'Were all the trees on earth to be made into pens, and the sea ink, with seven more seas yet added to it, the words of God would not be exhausted'. (31: 27) 'Say: "If the sea were ink for my Lord's words, the sea would surely dry up before my Lord's words are exhausted, even though we were to add to it another sea to replenish it"'. (18: 109) So, what is written with pens and what is not written is God's word and it is all the same.

Whoever says that God's word is a creature is an unbeliever, because God's speech is one of His attributes. He has distinguished between His creation and His words. He says: 'Your Lord is God who has created the heavens and the earth in six aeons, and is established on the throne. He covers the day with the night in swift pursuit. The sun, the moon and the stars are subservient to His command. Surely all creation and all authority belong to Him. Blessed is God, the Lord of the worlds'. (7: 54) In this verse, God distinguishes between His creation and His command. His creation includes those mentioned here: heavens, the earth, the sun, the moon and the stars, while His command is His speech with which He gives shape to His creatures, as He says in this verse: '[They are] subservient to His command'.

God created the voices of the reciters of the Qur'an just as He created their lips, tongues and throats as well as their movements, the air and their saliva. Yet this does not change the fact that what we hear from them is God's word. He says: 'Some of them would listen to the word of God then, having understood it, knowingly distort it?' (2: 75) This means that what is heard is God's word even though it is pronounced by the reciters. It is as some scholars said: 'The voice belongs to the reciter, but the word belongs to the Creator'.

CHAPTER EIGHT

'W'hen revealed text and rational thinking are combined together, religious truth is fully understood. Revealed text is of no benefit to one who has no reason, and reason on its own is of no help to one who has no knowledge of revelation. When either of these is missing knowledge of the truth is deficient. Should they superficially contradict each other revealed text is given precedence, because it comes from God's perfect knowledge while reason is derived from the knowledge of creatures, which is imperfect.

Reason is like the 'seeing sense' while the revealed text is like light. No one benefits by having two eyes when he is in pitch black darkness, just like a rational person benefits nothing by his reason without revelations. The better the light, the better the vision. Similarly, the more text is revealed the better reason is guided. When religious text and reason complement each other perfectly full guidance and insight are at their optimum, just like vision is at its best at midday. God says: 'Is he who was dead and whom We have raised to life and for whom We set up a light to see his way among men to be compared to one who is in deep darkness out of which he cannot emerge?' (6: 122)

A rational person benefits by reason in his life just like flying and walking animals benefit by their instincts. They migrate and settle at certain times, they know each other, find their way to their areas, make their own nests and recognize their predators.

However, man cannot find sufficient guidance from reason to know his Lord in full unless he benefits by what He has revealed to His messenger. Man simply cannot reach out to his Lord without the benefit of divine revelations, because without them he is in darkness: 'God is the patron of the believers. He leads them out of darkness into the light. As for the unbelievers, their patrons are false deities who lead them out of light into darkness. Those are the people destined for the Fire, therein to abide'. (2: 257)

We note that God says that He 'leads them', because without Him they will remain in darkness. Light is the same even though it may be of different types, such as fire and brightness. Likewise, revelation is the same even though it may be in different forms, such as the Qur'an and the Sunnah. God says: 'Believers, obey God and obey the messenger'. (4: 59)

A person who says that he will know God through his reason, without need of revelation, is the same as one who claims to find the right way using only his eyes, without the need for light. Both deny what is definitely necessary: the first has no religion and the second has no life.

God describes His revelations as light that gives guidance to all mankind: 'Those, therefore, who believe in him, honour and support him, and follow the light that has been bestowed from on high through him shall indeed be successful'. (7: 157) His revelations provide guidance to prophets and to their followers.

We accept what God has commanded and prohibited and we believe in what He has told us. If we know the reason for any particular thing we believe in it, but if we do not know it we still believe and submit. Reason does not necessarily comprehend every reasonable thing. How can it comprehend what is incomprehensible and how can all minds agree to it?

The one who says that he accepts those of God's laws and rulings that reason comprehends but disbelieves what is incomprehensible puts reason ahead of divine revelations. If our mind cannot comprehend something this does not mean it does not exist. It only means that it lies beyond our faculties of comprehension. The human mind has a limit beyond which it cannot go, just like eyesight has a limit. The furthest one can see does not represent the end of the universe or existence. Likewise, hearing has a limit but this does not mean the end of sound. An ant makes a sound that we cannot hear and similarly there are atmospheres, planets and stars in the universe that are invisible to us.

CHAPTER NINE

The authority to legislate belongs to God alone: He makes what He wills permissible or forbidden, according to His knowledge and infinite wisdom. His legislation is to ensure that both religion and life are on the proper course. His commands apply to all those who are subject to them and cannot be removed at any time or place without His permission.

We do not differentiate between His legislation for religion and life, they are both religious and for life. The religious ones include prayer, fasting, the pilgrimage, glorifying Him and attending mosques. Those that are concerned with human life include commercial transactions, marriage, divorce, inheritance, etc. Whoever distinguishes between the two, assigning judgement over religious matters to God and giving to someone other than God the authority to rule over worldly or life matters is an unbeliever. Judgement belongs to God alone and whoever assigns this authority to anyone else is in the same position as one who says that prostration may be offered by right to someone other than God. He says: 'All judgement rests with God alone'. (12: 40)

This was the way the Children of Israel became unbelievers, as God says: 'They make of their rabbis and their monks, and of the Christ, son of Mary, lords besides God. Yet they have been ordered to worship none but the One God, other than whom there is no deity. Exalted be He above those to whom they ascribe divinity'. (9: 31) In this verse God clearly describes their action as giving divinity to beings other than God.

God revealed His book and gave His legislation knowing what conditions will be like at all times and what had happened in the past. He also knew the exact situation at the time He bestowed His legislation from on high. His knowledge is not diminished because of an event that might have taken place in the past or may take place in the future. Nor is His knowledge increased because of an event that is happening at present. To Him, knowledge of the past, present and future is all the same. All glory be to Him.

Whoever believes that God's legislation was only suitable for the time when it was revealed and in future people may legislate for themselves what they feel suitable, even though it may be in conflict with God's legislation and judgement, is an unbeliever. Whoever says this starts from the premise that human knowledge of the present and what has not yet taken place is different, and as a result man's judgement will differ according to the difference in his knowledge. He imagines that this also applies to God and thus gives present human knowledge a higher position than that of God's knowledge at the time of revelation or what will happen in the future. This is blatant disbelief. God knows what is witnessed in the here and now in exactly the same way as He knows what is beyond the present. As He describes Himself: 'He knows all that is beyond the reach of human perception, and all that can be witnessed. Sublimely exalted is He above anything they associate as partner with Him'. (23: 92) His judgement applies to what is witnessed in the same way as it applies to what lies beyond our perception. He says: 'Say: "God! Originator of the heavens and the earth! You have knowledge of all that is beyond anyone's perception and all that anyone may witness. It is You who will judge between Your servants concerning all that over which they differ"'. (39: 46) His judgement applies to all His servants: those who are present and those who are not.

Whoever separates judgement on religious matters from that of life matters, assigning the first to God and giving man the authority to judge the latter, favours a multiplicity of legislators, while in fact God alone is the Legislator: 'Do you, then, believe in some parts of the Scriptures and deny others?' (2: 85) Whoever denies any part of God's book denies it all.

It is God's commandment that judgement between people should be on the basis of what He has revealed to His messenger of the Book and wisdom. As God says to His messenger: 'Hence, judge between them in accordance with what God has revealed and do not follow their vain desires, but beware of them lest they tempt you away from any part of what God has revealed to you'. (5: 49) The verse relates to judgement in disputes between people. The Prophet is warned against submitting to any temptation that leads him to deviate from God's judgement.

On questions where revelations do not give us any details competent scholars may deduce rulings, provided that the judgement they arrive at is not in conflict with any confirmed divine ruling.

People's judgement that is in conflict with God's ruling may not be given precedence. Had this been the case, prophets would have deviated from the truth. Prophets were sent to peoples who had already agreed among themselves what was contrary to the divine law, at least most of them, and in delivering their message prophets advocated what was contrary to the views of their communities.

CHAPTER TEN

God has assigned their lot to all creatures before they were created, and every creature was created by God's determination that preceded its creation. God says: 'It is He who has created all things and ordained them in due proportions'. (25: 2) 'We have created everything in due measure'. (54: 49) 'God's will is always destiny absolute'. (33: 38)

God has determined all matters and all things, good and bad. In an authentic *hadith* the Prophet states that an essential part of faith is 'to believe in divine destiny, both the good and the evil of it'.[3]

God's knowledge is essential for His determination of destiny. No one can determine things except the One who knows them. No one knows their fine details, places, changes, beginning and end except for their Creator. God says that we must learn that 'God has power over all things, and God encompasses all things with His knowledge'. (65: 12) 'How could it be that He who has created should not know all? He is above all comprehension, yet is All-Aware'. (67: 14)

Whoever denies God's determination of all things denies His knowledge, and whoever denies God's knowledge denies His determination. What God determined for His creation is all recorded in a book kept with Him. He says: 'No single thing have We left out of the book'. (6: 38) 'We keep an account of all things in a clear record'. (36: 12)

God's creation is of two types: 1) creatures that have no will of their own, such as planets and stars; and 2) creatures that have a will and freedom of choice, such as humans, jinn and angels. He has not set them on their respective courses without giving them a choice, so as to force them to disobey Him and then punish them for that. Nor did He give them total freedom without any aspect of subservience, so as to enable them to be His partners in will and action. He has given them a will that is under His will, as He says: 'This is only a reminder to all mankind, to those of you whose will is to be upright. Yet, you cannot will except by the will of God, Lord of all the worlds'. (82: 27–9)

---

3   Related by Muslim, 8.

God created people and their actions, as He says: 'Do you worship something that you yourselves have carved, while it is God who has created you and all you do?' (37: 95-6)) He created causes and determined their effects and this is the result of His perfect and complete knowledge as well as His infinite wisdom in establishing the universe in such a fine and perfect system.

It is not right for the human mind to turn away from believing in what it does not understand of God's wisdom or its essence of God's determination. The wisdom behind certain things may be beyond the capacity of our minds' comprehension. The human mind is like a vessel and some wisdom is like the water of the ocean. Should too much water be poured into this vessel it would drown it, leaving it completely lost, and the continued contemplation of some wisdom only increases man's perplexity, just like the sun at mid-day hurts our eyes if we stare fixedly at it.

CHAPTER ELEVEN

*D*eath is inevitable. God says: 'All that lives on it perishes; but forever will remain the face of your Lord, full of majesty, granting grace'. (55: 26–7) It is a part of faith that we should believe in what comes after death, including one's examination in the grave and the resulting happiness or torment.

Moreover, it is essential to believe in resurrection. God says: 'The Trumpet will be sounded and out of their graves they will rise and hasten to their Lord'. (36: 51) Whoever doubts the resurrection disbelieves in God: 'And as for the unbelievers, [they will be asked]: "When My revelations were recited to you, did you not glory in your arrogance and persist in your wicked ways? For when it was said, 'God's promise will certainly come true, and there can be no doubt about the Last Hour,' you would answer, 'We know nothing of the Last Hour. We think it is all conjecture, and we are by no means convinced'"'. (45: 31–2) Needless to say, the one who denies the Day of Judgement is also an unbeliever: 'Nay! It is the Last Hour that they deny. For those who deny the Last Hour We have prepared a blazing fire'. (25: 11)

Another part of faith is to believe in the reckoning on the Day of Judgement. God says: 'We shall set up just scales on the Day of Resurrection, so that no soul shall be wronged in the least. If there be but the weight of a mustard seed We shall bring it [to account]. Sufficient are We for reckoning'. (21: 47)

Yet another part of faith is to believe in reward and punishment, heaven and hell. God says: 'Those who will have brought wretchedness upon themselves, they will be in the Fire where they will sob and moan'. (11: 106) 'And those who are blessed with happiness will be in Paradise'. (11: 108) The unbelievers will go to the Fire and the believers will be in heaven, as God says: 'As for those who disbelieve I shall inflict on them severe suffering in this world and in the life to come; and they shall have none to help them. But to those who believe and do good works, He will grant their reward in full. God does not love the wrongdoers'. (3: 56-7)

It is also required to believe in everything stated in authentic texts of the things that will take place in the life to come and on the Day of Judgement, such as the pathway, the scales, the pond and the scrolls of people's good and evil deeds.[4]

---

[4] The pathway is a sort of bridge that is erected over Hell on the Day of Judgement. All people will need to cross it in order to reach Heaven. Believers will be able to do so, while unbelievers will fall. The scales are placed to weigh people's actions which they did during their life on earth. The pond belongs to Prophet Muhammad when he will give people to drink. Only believers may drink from it. The scrolls are records of all that people do in this present life. Each one will be handed their records on the Day of Judgement and the believers will be proud of their records calling on other people to look into them. The unbelievers will wish that they had never seen their records.

CHAPTER TWELVE

To stay with the community is obligatory and no community exists without a leader, or imam. The leader of the Muslim community is obeyed in line with the obedience of God, who says: 'Believers, obey God and obey the messenger and those from among you who have been entrusted with authority'. (4: 59) The phrase, 'from among you,' means from among the Muslims. An unbeliever may not be an imam nor a leader of the Muslim community, nor is it permissible to appoint an unbeliever to such a post. It is not required to obey him except insofar as what serves the interests of the community.

If the leader of the Muslim community does not have good knowledge of Islam he should appoint a scholar to advise him, so as to ensure that the religious and worldly affairs of the Muslim community are set on the right basis: 'If any matter pertaining to peace or war comes to their knowledge, they make it known to all and sundry; whereas, if they would only refer it to the Messenger and to those from among them entrusted with authority, those of them who are engaged in obtaining intelligence would know it'. (4: 83)

It is not permissible to rebel against the leader or try to usurp his authority. If he deals unfairly his unfairness should be tolerated with resignation, unless he perpetrates some clear unbelief. Umm Salamah, the Prophet's wife, reports that the Prophet said: 'Some leaders will be appointed over you and you shall be happy with some of their actions but not with others. Whoever is displeased with the latter clears himself of responsibility, and whoever speaks out against it is safe. It is the one who accepts and follows [that is condemned]'. People asked: 'Messenger of God, should we not fight them?' He said: 'Not as long as they attend to their prayers'.[5]

Advice should be offered to the ruler with knowledge and wisdom, so as to remove or lessen evil. Such advice should not be aimed to seek self-satisfaction or to show the ruler in a bad light. In an authentic *hadith* the Prophet said: 'Religion is sincere counsel'. We said: 'To whom'? [The Prophet] said: 'To God, His Book, His messenger, and to the leaders of the Muslims and their common folk'.[6]

---

5   Related by Muslim, 1854.
6   Related by Muslim, 55.

A scholar must not stay away from people's affairs without concerning himself with what sets their affairs on the right course. If he does not seek life's comforts, so as to personally stay away from temptation, then this is good and praiseworthy. However, if he does not concern himself with people's affairs his attitude is not the right one. Indeed, he should support whoever suffers injustice, even if his support is merely offering what is very little when he cannot afford more. He should seek help in order to feed the hungry, even if it yields no more than a date. A scholar has recognized authority and setting people's life on the right basis serves as a way to improve their religious attitude. The Prophet never aspired to any riches even when the treasures of the earth were available to him, but he supported Barirah and others over the case of a few dinars, even delivering a speech about the case.

CHAPTER THIRTEEN

Jihad continues until the end of human life and remains in force all of the time, as long as the Qur'an remains. In an authentic hadith, Jabir reports that the Prophet said: 'A group of my community will continue to fight for the truth, prevailing until the Day of Judgement'.[7]

When jihad is to repel an attacking enemy it does not require permission by the leader or the formulation of the right intention. It is sufficient that it is undertaken to remove and repel harm and aggression. It is obligatory, even if it is to defend one's honour, life or property. According to the *hadith*: 'Whoever is killed defending his property is a martyr, and whoever is killed defending his family, himself or his faith is a martyr'.[8] The *hadith* is given in a shorter form in the two Sahih anthologies.[9]

It is a duty to repel an aggressor in defence of one's honour, self or property, whether the aggressor is a Muslim or an unbeliever. 'A man came to the Prophet and said: "What should I do if a man comes aiming to take my property?" The Prophet said: "Remind him of God". The man said: "Suppose he turns a deaf ear?" The Prophet said: "Then seek the help of those Muslims who are close to you?" The man said: "What if there is no Muslim close by?" The Prophet said: "Then seek the help of government authority?" The man said: "And if the authority takes no action to help me?" The Prophet said: "Then fight to protect your property until you are either killed and be a martyr or you keep your property safe"'.[10]

When the Muslim community is on the offensive the intention must be to make God's word supreme. An authentic *hadith*, reported by Abu Musa al-Ash[ari, states: 'A Bedouin came to the Prophet and asked: "Messenger of God: a man fights for a share of war gains, and one fights so as to gain a reputation, and one fights so that he is seen. Which of these is considered for God's cause?" The Prophet said: "He who fights so that God's word is supreme is fighting for God's cause"'.[11]

---

7   Related by Muslim, 156.
8   Related by Abu Dawud, 4772; al-Tirmidhi, 1421; al-Nasa'i, 4095 and Ibn Majah, 2580 on the authority of Sa[id ibn Zayd.
9   Related by al-Bukhari, 2348; Muslim, 141 on the authority of [Abdullah ibn [Amr.
10 Related by al-Nasa'i, 4081; Ibn Abi Shaybah, 28043; Ahmad, 22514; al-Tabarani in Al-Mu[jam al-Kabir, vol. 20, p. 313.
11 Related by al-Bukhari, 123 and 2655; Muslim, 1904.

In jihad, it is obligatory to obey the leader of the Muslim community provided that he does not order anything that is forbidden in Islam. The Prophet said: 'Whoever obeys me obeys God, and whoever disobeys me disobeys God. Whoever obeys the commander I appoint obeys me, and whoever disobeys the commander I appoint disobeys me'.[12]

---

12 Related by al-Bukhari, 6718; Muslim, 1835 on Abu Hurayrah's authority.

CHAPTER FOURTEEN

The best of people are prophets, then Prophet Muhammad's companions. Their high status is stated in the Qur'an: 'Muhammad is God's Messenger; and those who are with him are firm and unyielding towards the unbelievers, full of mercy towards one another. You can see them bowing down, prostrating in prayer, seeking favour with God and His good pleasure'. (48: 29)

Just like some prophets are of a higher standard than others, the Prophet's companions are of different standards. The lowest ranking prophet is superior to the highest ranking companion of the Prophet. Likewise, the lowest ranking companion of the Prophet is superior to the highest ranking person among the following generations.

The best of the Prophet's companions were those who believed in Islam during the early days of the religion. The one who believed in the Prophet's message during the time when Islam was in a position of weakness is better than those who believed during Islam's time of strength. Certainly, those who believed before Makkah fell to Islam are better than those who believed after its fall. God says: 'Those of you who gave and fought [for God's cause] before the victory are not like the others: they are higher in rank than those who gave and fought afterwards'. (57: 10) However, the merit of companionship with the Prophet is assured to those who believed afterwards. The Qur'anic verse goes on to say: 'Although God has promised the ultimate good to all of them. God is well aware of all that you do'. (57: 10) God also says: 'As for the first to lead the way, of the Muhajirin and the Ansar, as well as those who follow them in [the way of] righteousness, God is well-pleased with them, and well-pleased are they with Him'. (9: 100)

The best of the earliest believers are the ten to whom the Prophet gave the happy news of being in heaven, and the best of these are the four Caliphs. Next to these ten are the Prophet's companions who fought in the Battle of Badr, and next to them are those who fought in the Battle of Uhud, then come those who gave their pledges to the Prophet under the tree. God says: 'God was indeed well pleased with the believers when they pledged their allegiance to you under the tree. He knew what was in their hearts and so He sent down tranquillity upon them and rewarded them with a speedy victory'. (48: 18) In an authentic *hadith*, Jabir reports that the Prophet said to those who gave their pledges under the tree: 'You are the best of people on earth'.[13] They were fourteen hundred.

The Prophet's companions were the trustees of God's revelations and they delivered Islam to people. To speak ill of them is to cut the transmission of Islam and to raise doubts about the Sunnah of the final messenger of God. They are indeed the safeguards of the Muslim community after the Prophet, as stated clearly in an authentic *hadith*: 'My companions are safeguards for my community: when they are gone, my community will face what is in store for it'.[14]

The Prophet's companions were not infallible. However, their mistakes should never be an excuse to attack them. Their disagreements should not be revived, except for learning from and drawing lessons. Therefore, it should be looked into with respect and not for seeking excuses. Even when they disagreed, the Prophet's companions were better than other people, even though they might be in agreement. God has granted them their high status because of their good companionship of the Prophet, not because of their companionship with one another. Therefore, their disagreement with one another was a question of choices when they all endeavoured to be right and they are rewarded for their choices even if these were wrong. To claim that they disagreed with the Prophet is to be unjust to them and God has cleared them of it. They gave the Prophet good companionship and through him they were better than other people.

To criticise the Prophet's companions is risky, because this is an area that will grow wider and wider. If criticism is levelled at one of them it will open the way to criticism of others, hence the *tabi*[*in* and their followers refrained from it. [Umar ibn [Abd al-[Aziz was asked about [Ali, [Uthman and the Battles of the Camel and Siffin and what happened during that period. His answer was: 'These led to the shedding of blood and God has spared my hand from these. I will not dip my tongue in them'.[15]

No one who comes after them will be questioned on their disagreements on the Day of Judgement, but everyone will be asked whether they recognized their merits.

---

13 Related by al-Bukhari, 4154.
14 Related by Muslim, 2531.
15 Ibn Sa[d, *Al-Tabaqat al-Kubra*, vol. 5, p. 394; Ibn [Asakir, *Tarikh Dimashq*, vol. 65, p. 133.

CHAPTER FIFTEEN

'We do not call anyone who offers the Islamic prayer an unbeliever as a result of committing any sin other than disbelief in God. To revile God is an act of disbelief and is indeed worse than associating partners with him. An idolater does not bring God down to the status of stones; rather he elevates the stones to the rank of God. God mentions in the Qur'an what unbelievers will say on the Day of Judgement: 'By God, we were obviously in error when we deemed you equal to the Lord of all the worlds'. (26: 97-8) The one who reviles God brings Him down below the rank of stones.

To revile God is very grave disbelief. Like faith, disbelief may decrease and increase. God says: 'The postponement [of sacred months] is only an excess of unbelief'. (9: 37) 'But those who return to disbelief after having accepted the faith and then grow more stubborn in their rejection of the faith, their repentance will not be accepted. For they are those who have truly gone astray'. (3: 90) However, the increase or decrease of disbelief does not lead to the unbeliever becoming exempt from punishment in the Fire; it only leads to increasing or lessening his punishment. God says: 'Upon those who disbelieve and debar others from the path of God, We will heap suffering upon suffering in punishment for all the corruption they wrought'. (16: 88)

We do not testify that any particular person will be in heaven or hell except those whom God and His messenger have stated their destiny. We bear witness that whoever dies a believer belongs to heaven and whoever dies unbeliever will be in the Fire.

CHAPTER SIXTEEN

The essence of freedom is to be free of subservience to anyone other than God. To think that freedom is to discard God's commandments is nothing less than considering oneself as the idol and giving subservience to desire. God says: 'Consider the one who takes his own desires as his deity, and whom God has [therefore] let go astray despite his knowledge [of the truth], sealing his ears and heart and placing a cover on his eyes: who can guide such a person after God [has abandoned him]? Will you not, then, take heed?' (45: 23)

Whoever justifies that man can do and say whatever he chooses, as he chooses and when he chooses, accepts that man is subservient to his own desire. Man is created as a subservient being: if he does not submit himself to God and worship Him, he will worship someone else, without doubt.

Had there been only one human being living on earth, God would not have legislated for him punishment for murder, false accusation and adultery; nor would He have required him to lower his gaze or to adopt a system of inheritance. He would not have forbidden him adultery, usury and other vile practices. God has legislated all these because man lives with other human beings. The greater the number of people, the more life needs controls. Had the moon been the only one in space would God have assigned it such an accurate existence? He has made it move so accurately in order to be part of the system that includes the sun, the earth, the planets and other celestial bodies. The greater their number the more control is required.

God says: 'He covers the day with the night in swift pursuit. The sun, the moon and the stars are subservient to His command. Surely all creation and all authority belong to Him. Blessed is God, the Lord of the worlds'. (7: 54) 'Neither can the sun overtake the moon, nor can the night outrun the day. Each floats in its own orbit'. (36: 40) Islamic legislation is meant to regulate matters of religion and life. Whoever justifies violating God's laws for himself incurs His punishment.

To embrace Islam is obligatory and to turn away from it is apostasy. As God says: 'Whoever of you renounces his faith and dies an unbeliever, his works shall come to nothing in this world and in the world to come. Such people are destined for hell, wherein they shall abide'. (2: 217) The Prophet says: 'Whoever changes his religion should be killed'.[16]

To worship God is the ultimate purpose of creation and existence. Whoever allows himself to be turned away from it does not believe that it is the purpose of existence. How is it that a person prohibits the breach of the constitution or the laws of one's country but justifies the breach of submission to God? To do so is to implicitly admit that one does not truly believe in the purpose of creation. But God says: 'I have not created the jinn and mankind to any end other than that they may worship Me'. (51: 56)

The One who brought the humans and the jinn into this life to worship Him alone will certainly bring them into the life to come, so that they will account for their deeds and receive their reward or punishment.

May God grant us the best of situations in life and give us the best of provisions.

Peace and blessings be upon His prophet and those who follow him.

---

16 Related by al-Bukhari, 2854.

IslamHouse.com

eDialogue

Interested in ISLAM?
Join For a Free Private Live Chat

edialogue org

For more details visit
www.GuideToIslam.com

contact us :Books@guidetoislam.com

عـرض تعـريـف عــن مركـز أصــول
ومجالاته ووحداته.. مشاهدة ممتعة لك

www.osoulcenter.com

To Download This Book, please Visit:

 OSOUL STORE

www.ingramcontent.com/pod-product-compliance
Lightning Source LLC
LaVergne TN
LVHW050142080526
838202LV00062B/6561